Quality Standards

for

Federal Offices of Inspector General

Council of the Inspectors General on Integrity and Efficiency

August 2012

Foreword

In anticipation of the fourth anniversary of the creation of tThe Council of the Inspectors General on Integrity and Efficiency (CIGIE), its members have updated the *Quality Standards for Federal Offices of Inspector General*. The standards in the Silver Book set forth the overall quality framework for managing, operating, and conducting the work of Offices of Inspector General and will guide the Inspector General Community's efforts into the future.

The Honorable Phyllis K. Fong
Chairperson, CIGIE

Mr. Carl A. Clinefelter
Vice Chairperson, CIGIE

Contents

Quality Standards for Federal Offices of Inspector General

I. Introduction

A. Purpose

This document contains quality standards for the management, operation, and conduct of the Federal Offices of Inspector General (OIG). Executive Order 12805 gave the President's Council on Integrity and Efficiency (PCIE) and the Executive Council on Integrity and Efficiency (ECIE)[1] the responsibility for developing professional standards for OIGs.[2] The Inspector General Reform Act of 2008 (IG Reform Act) created the Council of the Inspectors General on Integrity and Efficiency (CIGIE), which combined the PCIE and ECIE into a single council.[3] The members of CIGIE have formulated and adopted these standards. They are for OIG use to guide the conduct of official duties in a professional manner. These standards incorporate by reference the existing professional standards for audit, investigation, and inspection and evaluation efforts.

Public office carries with it a responsibility to apply and account for the use of public resources economically,

---

[1] Executive Order 12805, dated May 11, 1992, updated the charter for the President's Council on Integrity and Efficiency and created the Executive Council on Integrity and Efficiency.
[2] Executive Order 12805, Section 3(c), states that individual members of the Councils should, to the extent permitted under law, adhere to professional standards developed by the Councils. This section gives the Councils the authority to establish standards for quality.
[3] 5 U.S.C. app. 3 § 11.

efficiently, and effectively.[4] The OIGs have a special need for high standards of professionalism and integrity in light of the mission of the Inspectors General under the Act.[5] Because of this special need, the CIGIE has adopted the general quality standards contained in this document.

B. OIG Mission

OIGs have responsibility to report on current performance and accountability and to foster sound program management to help ensure effective government operations. The Inspector General Act of 1978, as amended (IG Act), created the OIGs to:[6]

1. Conduct, supervise, and coordinate audits and investigations relating to the programs and operations of their agencies;

2. Review existing and proposed legislation and regulations to make recommendations concerning the impact of such legislation and regulations on economy and efficiency or the prevention and detection of fraud and abuse;

---

[4] *The Standards for Internal Control in the Federal Government*, published by the U.S. General Accounting Office (GAO) in November 1999, require that "Management and employees should establish and maintain an environment throughout the organization that sets a positive and supportive attitude toward internal control and conscientious management." The Internal Control Standards define internal control as an integral component of an organization's management that provides reasonable assurance that the following objectives are being achieved: (1) effectiveness and efficiency of operations, (2) reliability of financial reporting, and (3) compliance with applicable laws and regulations.

[5] The IG Act (Public Law 95-452), Section 2, established *independent and objective units* to review agency activities.

[6] 5 U.S.C. app. 3 §§ 2 and 4.

3. Provide leadership for activities designed to promote economy, efficiency, and effectiveness, and to promote efforts to reduce fraud, waste, and abuse in the programs and operations of their agencies;

4. Coordinate relationships between the agency and other Federal agencies, State and local government agencies, and non-government agencies to promote economy and efficiency, to prevent and detect fraud and abuse, or to identify and prosecute participants engaged in fraud or abuse;

5. Inform their agency heads and Congress of problems in their agencies' programs and operations and the necessity for and progress of corrective actions; and

6. Report to the Attorney General whenever the Inspector General has reasonable grounds to believe there has been a violation of Federal criminal law.

In addition to audits and investigations referenced above, OIGs may conduct, supervise, and coordinate inspections, evaluations, and other reviews related to the programs and operations of their departments and agencies. The IG Reform Act recognized the longstanding practice of the IG community to also conduct inspections and evaluations.[7]

C. Relationship to Federal Laws and Regulations, and Federal and Professional Standards

OIG operations are subject to a variety of Federal laws and regulations, and Federal and other professional standards, such as the IG Act, Single Audit Act, *Standards of Ethical Conduct for Employees of the Executive Branch*, the *Government*

---

[7] 5 U.S.C. app. 3 § 11(b), (c).

Auditing Standards, the CIGIE *Quality Standards for Inspection and Evaluation*, and the CIGIE *Quality Standards for Investigations*. The standards contained in this document are derived from these and other requirements. These standards, however, are not intended to contradict or supersede applicable standards or Federal laws and regulations. See Appendix I for a list of major laws, regulations, and standards that apply to OIGs.

An OIG may be a component of an entity that is not legally defined as a "Federal agency." For this, or other reasons, certain laws, regulations, or other guidance cited in this document may not be directly applicable to certain OIGs. Where a standard contained in this document is premised on law or other criteria not directly applicable to an OIG, OIGs are encouraged to adopt the underlying principles and concepts to their operations where appropriate and feasible.

II. Ethics, Independence, and Confidentiality

A. General Standards[8]

The Inspector General (IG) and Office of Inspector General staff shall adhere to the highest ethical principles by conducting their work with integrity.[9]

Integrity is the cornerstone of all ethical conduct, ensuring adherence to accepted codes of ethics and practice. Objectivity, independence, professional judgment, and confidentiality are all elements of integrity.

Objectivity imposes the obligation to be impartial, intellectually honest, and free of conflicts of interest.

Independence is a critical element of objectivity. Without independence, both in fact and in appearance, objectivity is impaired.

Professional judgment requires working with competence and diligence. Competence is a combination of education and experience and involves a commitment to learning and professional improvement. Professional standards for audits, investigations, and inspections and evaluations require

---

[8] This standard was adapted from the *Standards for Ethical Conduct for Employees of the Executive Branch,* the American Institute of Certified Public Accountants' Code of Professional Conduct, Section ET 53-56, and the Institute of Internal Auditors' Code of Ethics.

[9] 5 U.S.C. app. 3 § 2, established independent units to review agency activities. Section 6(a)(2) gives the Inspector General responsibility for independently determining the nature and extent of the work necessary.

continuing professional education (see the Managing Human Capital standard). Diligence requires that services be rendered promptly, carefully, and thoroughly, and by observing the applicable professional and ethical standards.

Confidentiality requires respecting the value and ownership of privileged, sensitive, or classified information received and protecting that information, and safeguarding the identity of confidential informants. In some instances, legal or professional obligations may require an OIG to disclose information it has received.

B. Standards for Ethical Conduct for Employees of the Executive Branch

The IG and OIG staff should follow the *Standards for Ethical Conduct for Employees of the Executive* Branch[10] (Ethical Standards) and the Federal conflict of interest laws.[11] These standards guide the Inspector General and the OIG staff to respect and adhere to the 14 principles of ethical conduct, as well as the implementing standards contained in the Ethical Standards and in supplemental agency regulations. The first principle emphasizes that public service is a public trust,

---

[10] Codified in 5 C.F.R. Part 2635. These regulations do not apply to all IG offices. Nonetheless, those offices for which these regulations do not apply should adhere generally to the principles and standards enunciated in these regulations and establish policies to reflect such adherence.

[11] 18 U.S.C. §§ 202-209. These statutory provisions apply to officers or employees of the executive or legislative branch of the United States Government, of any independent agency of the United States or of the District of Columbia; thus they may not technically apply to certain Designated FFederal Entities . Nonetheless, those DFEs are encouraged and should adhere generally to the principles and standards enunciated in these statutes and establish policies to reflect such adherence.

requiring employees to place loyalty to the Constitution, laws, and ethical principles above private gain.

An independent mechanism for resolving allegations against inspectors general and designated OIG senior staff is established under the IG Reform Act. The IG Reform Act established that the Integrity Committee (IC) of the Council of the Inspectors General on Integrity and Efficiency (CIGIE) is responsible for receiving, reviewing, and referring for investigation, where appropriate, allegations of administrative (non-criminal) misconduct or wrongdoing against Inspectors General, and designated senior staff members of the OIG.

An Inspector General shall refer to the IC any allegation of wrongdoing against staff members of the office of that IG who report directly to the IG (or those who are designated as such, under CIGIE guidelines),[12] if review of the substance of the allegation cannot be assigned to an agency of the executive branch with appropriate jurisdiction over the matter and the IG determines that an objective internal investigation of the allegation is not feasible or an internal investigation of the allegation may appear not to be objective.

CIGIE has established a "Threshold Standard" to be considered before the IC will further review the allegation. The Threshold Standard is defined as a violation of any law, rule or regulation, or gross mismanagement, gross waste of funds or abuse of authority, or conduct so serious that it may undermine the

---

[12] Each IG is required to designate those positions on its staff who qualify as "staff members" subject to review by the CIGIE Integrity Committee. See 5 U.S.C. app. 3 § 11(d)(4)(C) and CIGIE, *Integrity Committee Policy and Procedures* (April 2009), Section 4.

independence or integrity reasonably expected of an IG or OIG senior staff member.[13]

OIGs should maintain policies and controls to ensure that allegations are handled consistent with the IG Act and CIGIE standards.

Where a situation is not covered by a specific standard set forth in the Ethical Standards or in supplemental agency regulations, the Inspector General and OIG staff shall apply the principles underlying the standards in determining whether their planned or actual conduct is proper.[14] OIG staff should also consult with the Designated Agency Ethics Official or similar official within their office, agency or organization regarding application of the Ethical Standards.

C. Independence

The IG and OIG staff must be free both in fact and appearance from personal, external, and organizational impairments to independence. The IG and OIG staff has a responsibility to maintain independence, so that opinions, conclusions, judgments, and recommendations will be impartial and will be viewed as impartial by knowledgeable third parties. The IG and OIG staff should avoid situations that could lead reasonable third parties with knowledge of the relevant facts and circumstances to conclude that the OIG is not able to maintain independence in conducting its work.

---

[13] *Integrity Committee Policy and Procedures*, Section 8.
[14] 5 C.F.R. § 2635.101(b).

1. Statutory Independence

The IG Act established OIGs to create organizationally independent and objective units. This statutory independence is intended to ensure the integrity and objectivity of OIG activities. The IG Act authorizes IGs to:

a. Conduct such audits and investigations, and issue such reports, as they believe appropriate (with limited national security and law enforcement exceptions).[15]

b. Issue subpoenas for information and documents outside the agency (with the same limited exceptions).[16]

c. Have direct access to all records and information of the agency.[17]

d. Have ready access to the agency head.[18]

e. Administer oaths for taking testimony.[19]

f. Hire and control their own staff and contract resources.[20]

g. Request assistance from any Federal, state or local governmental agency or unit.[21]

h. Have separate legal counsel.[22]

IGs report to both the head of their respective agencies and to the Congress.[23] This dual reporting responsibility is the

---

[15] 5 U.S.C. app. 3 § 2 and 4.
[16] *Id.* at § 6(a)(4).
[17] *Id.* at § 6(a)(1).
[18] *Id.* at § 6(a)(6).
[19] *Id.* at § 6(a)(5).
[20] *Id.* at § 6(a)(7), (8), and (9).
[21] *Id.* at § 6(a)(3).
[22] *Id.* at § 6.

framework within which Inspectors General perform their functions. Unique in government, dual reporting is the legislative safety net that protects the I G's independence and objectivity.

2. Conceptual Framework for Independence

In all matters relating to audit work, the audit organization and the individual auditor, whether government or the public, must be independent. In conducting its work, OIG staff must be both independent in fact and in appearance. This requires staff to act with integrity and exercise objectivity and professional skepticism and avoid circumstances that would cause a reasonable and informed third party to believe that staff is not capable of exercising objective and impartial judgment or that an OIG's work had been compromised.[24]

The steps to assessing OIG independence are as follows:

    a. identify threats to independence;
    b. evaluate the significance of the threats identified, both individually and in the aggregate; and
    c. apply safeguards as necessary to eliminate the threats or reduce them to an acceptable level.

Threats to Independence:

---

[23] *Id.* at §§ 2(3), 4(a)(5), and 5(b).
[24] The standards in this part are adapted from *GAGAS Internet version* (August 2011), Chapter 3.

There are generally seven categories of threats that may apply to OIG work:

1. Self-interest: the threat that a financial or other interest will inappropriately influence an auditor's judgment or behavior;
2. Self-review: the threat that an OIG employee or OIG that has provided non-audit services will not appropriately evaluate the results of previous judgments made or services performed as part of the non-audit services when forming a judgment significant to an audit;
3. Bias: the threat that an OIG employee will, as a result of political, ideological, social, or other convictions, take a position that is not objective;
4. Familiarity: the threat that aspects of a relationship with management or personnel of an audited entity, such as a close or long relationship, or that of an immediate or close family member, will lead an OIG employee to take a position that is not objective;
5. Undue influence: the threat that external influences or pressures will impact an OIG employee's ability to make independent and objective judgments;
6. Management participation: the threat that results from an auditor's taking on the role of management or otherwise performing management functions on behalf of the entity undergoing an audit; and
7. Structural: the threat that an OIG's placement within a government entity, in combination with the structure of the government entity

being audited, will impact the OIG's ability to perform work and report results objectively.

Safeguards:

Safeguards are controls designed to eliminate or reduce threats to an acceptable level, but vary with the specific facts and circumstances under which threats to independence exist.[25] Safeguards may exist or develop from various sources, both external and internal. Several noted external safeguards are created by legislation, regulation, or applicable professional governing bodies. Internal safeguards are created generally pursuant to OIG policies and practices or entity directives. Examples of internal safeguards include but are not limited to: (1) OIG selection of a replacement non-impaired auditor, (2) utilizing separate engagement teams to avoid threats to independence, (3) implementing secondary reviews, and (4) involving another OIG or audit organization to perform or re-perform part of an audit.

OIGs should evaluate threats to independence both individually and in the aggregate because threats can have a cumulative effect on an OIG employee's independence. In cases where threats to independence of OIG work are not at an acceptable level, thereby requiring the application of safeguards, the OIG should document the threats identified and the safeguards applied to eliminate the threats or reduce them to an acceptable level.[26]

---

[25] *GAGAS (2011)* Section 3.16 – 3.19.

[26] For a fuller discussion of personal and external impairments, see *Government Auditing Standards (2007), also referred to as "Generally Accepted Government Auditing Standards," "GAGAS" or "Yellow*

OIGs should have policies and procedures in place to resolve, report, and document impairments to independence when they exist.

3. Types of Services

Auditors and audit organizations within OIGs have a specific independence standard required by the *Government Auditing Standards*.[27] This independence standard requires that, while auditors have the capability of performing a range of services for their clients, in some circumstances it is not appropriate for them to perform both audit and certain non-audit services for the same client.[28] The standard is based on two overarching principles:

a. Auditors should not perform management functions or make management decisions; and

b. Auditors should not audit their own work or provide non-audit services in situations where the amounts or services involved are significant and/or material to the subject matter of the audit.

For non-audit services OIGs should avoid assuming management responsibilities, such as setting policies, designing, implementing, or maintaining internal controls, performing routine management activities, and serving as a voting member of the audited entity's management committee or board of directors. An auditor who previously performed

---

Book") GAO, 2011 Sections 3.07 - 3.09 and 3.10;
Quality Standards for Inspections and Evaluations at 4-6.

[27] *Government Auditing Standards*, Sections 3.11 and 3.25
[28] GAGAS, Sections 3.33-3.58.

non-audit services for an entity that is a prospective subject of an audit should evaluate the impact of those non-audit services on independence before accepting an audit.[29]

In addition to its application to OIG audit activities, the first overarching principle should be applied broadly to all OIG activities. Specifically, OIG staff, and others under OIG direction, should not perform management functions or make management decisions for their agency.

Some services, by their nature, always impair an auditor's independence with respect to an audited entity, including determining or changing journal entries, account codes, or classifications for transactions; authorizing or approving the entity's transactions; preparing or making changes to source documents without management approval; preparing the audited entity's financial statements, and ongoing internal control monitoring. Other services, however, may be performed, provided that proper safeguards are implemented, such as evaluations of control effectiveness.

OIG audit organizations should take steps to ensure that auditors under contract to the OIG do not have independence impairments.

4. Conflicting Financial Interests

An OIG staff member's objectivity and independence may also be affected by personal financial interests that are held by the staff member or by certain family members, or by positions the staff member holds as a trustee, director, officer, or employee of an outside organization. OIG staff should notify appropriate officials within their organization if they or others within the organization have a potentially conflicting financial interest.

---

[29] GAGAS (2011) Sections 3.42 - 3.53.

D. Confidentiality

Each OIG shall safeguard the identity of confidential sources and protect privileged, confidential, and national security or classified information in compliance with applicable laws, regulations, and professional standards.[30] In addition, OIG staff shall not use confidential information for personal gain or in any other manner that is detrimental to the legitimate interests of the organization.[31] Congress has provided specific authority for withholding the identities of agency employees who make complaints to the OIG. Under Section 7 of the IG Act of 1978, as amended, the OIG may receive and investigate complaints or information from employees concerning the possible existence of an activity constituting a violation of law, rules, or regulations; mismanagement; waste of funds; abuse of authority; or a substantial and specific danger to the public health or safety. The IG shall not, after receipt of such complaint or information, disclose the identity of the agency employee without the consent of the employee, unless the IG determines that such disclosure is unavoidable during the course of the investigation..

The Freedom of Information Act, the Privacy Act, the Civil Service Reform Act, the Health Insurance Portability and Accountability Act,[32] the Trade Secrets Act,[33] and other Federal statutes and case law provide certain protections for the identities of sources and for sensitive information obtained.

---

[30] In maintaining confidentiality, OIGs should remain cognizant that records and information are also maintained in various electronic media.

[31] Institute of Internal Auditors' Code of Ethics, Principle 3.2.

[32] 42 U.S.C. § 1320d-2 and implementing regulations cover the privacy of individually identifiable health information.

[33] 18 U.S.C. § 1905 prohibits OIGs from disclosing confidential proprietary data obtained during the course of conducting their work unless such disclosure is authorized by law.

Additionally, the relevant professional standards provide guidance on the use, protection, and reporting of privileged and confidential information. OIGs must follow the guidance contained in these authorities.

III. Professional Standards

A. General Standard

Each OIG shall conduct, supervise, and coordinate its audits, investigations, inspections, and evaluations in compliance with the applicable professional standards listed below.

For audits:

Government Auditing Standards, issued by the U.S. Government Accountability Office (GAO).

For investigations:

Quality Standards for Investigations, accepted by CIGIE and consistent with applicable Department of Justice guidelines, and case law.

For inspections and evaluations:

Quality Standards for Inspection and Evaluation, accepted by CIGIE, *Government Auditing Standards*, or other appropriate professional standards.

IV. Ensuring Internal Control

A. General Standard

The IG and OIG staff shall direct and control OIG operations consistent with the *Standards for Internal Control in the Federal Government*[34] issued by the GAO. These standards require that internal control be part of an entity's management infrastructure to provide reasonable assurance that (1) operations are efficient and effective; (2) financial reporting is reliable; and (3) operations are in compliance with applicable laws, regulations, and professional standards.

Internal control is a continuous built-in component of operations, effected by people, that provides reasonable but not absolute assurance, that the OIG's objectives will be met. Internal control considerations include the following:

B. Efficient and Effective Operations

OIGs should strive to conduct their operation in the most efficient and effective manner. Each OIG should manage available resources at the least cost to produce the greatest results in terms of public benefit, return on investment, and risk reduction. OIGs derive much of their credibility to perform their work by demonstrating the ability to efficiently and effectively use and account for public funds.

---

[34] The Federal Managers' Financial Integrity Act of 1982 requires GAO to issue standards for internal control in government. The Office of Management and Budget issues implementing guidelines and specific requirements.

C. Control Environment

OIG management and staff should establish and maintain an environment throughout the organization that fosters a positive and supportive attitude toward internal control and conscientious management. Key factors affecting the control environment include the following:

1. Integrity and ethical values maintained and demonstrated by OIG management and staff, the organizational structure and delegations of authority and responsibility, and OIG management's philosophy and operating style.

2. OIG management's commitment to competence and human capital policies and practices (see the Managing Human Capital standard).

3. OIG management's relationship with the Congress, their agency, and the Office of Management and Budget (OMB).

D. Risk Assessment

The IG should provide for an assessment of the risks the OIG faces from both external and internal sources. Risk assessment includes identifying and analyzing relevant risks associated with achieving the OIG's objectives, such as those defined in strategic and annual performance plans, and forming a basis for determining how risks should be managed. Risk assessment methodologies and the formality of their documentation may vary from OIG to OIG, depending on the OIG's size, mission, and other factors.

E. Control Activities

The IG should establish and implement internal control activities that ensure the OIG's directives are carried out. The control activities should be effective and efficient in accomplishing the OIG's control objectives.

Control activities are the policies, procedures, techniques, and mechanisms that enforce management's directives. Control activities are an integral part of the planning, implementing, reviewing, and accountability activities. Control activities include supervisory reviews at all levels to ensure compliance with applicable professional standards, controls over information processing, physical control over vulnerable assets, establishing and reviewing performance measures and indicators, and segregation of duties.

F. Information and Communication

The IG should ensure that information is recorded and communicated to internal OIG management and others within the OIG who need it and in a form and within a time frame that enables them to carry out their internal quality control and other responsibilities.

For the OIG to control its operations, it must have relevant, reliable, and timely communications relating to internal and external events. Information is needed throughout the OIG to achieve all of its objectives.

G. Monitoring

The IG should ensure that monitoring assesses the quality of performance over time and ensures that the findings and recommendations of quality assurance and other reviews are promptly resolved.

The monitoring standard discusses three different types of activities: ongoing monitoring, self-assessment evaluations, and quality assurance reviews. Ongoing monitoring occurs in the course of normal operations and is continuous. Self-assessment evaluations and independent external reviews can be useful in focusing directly on the controls' effectiveness at a specific time.[35] The scope and frequency of these independent reviews should depend primarily on the assessment of risks and the effectiveness of ongoing control monitoring procedures.

1. *Ongoing monitoring* occurs in the course of normal operations. It is performed continually and is ingrained in the agency operations. It includes regular management and supervisory activities,[36] comparisons, reconciliations, and other actions employees take in performing their duties. Ongoing monitoring should include policies and procedures for ensuring that the findings of separate quality control evaluations and quality assurance reviews are promptly resolved.

2. *Self-assessment evaluations*, conducted by the unit or activity itself, include a reassessment of the risks associated with a particular activity and can include periodic reviews of control design and direct testing of

---

[35] The *Standards for Internal Control in the Federal Government* state that "Separate evaluations of control can also be useful by focusing directly on the controls' effectiveness at a specific time. The scope and frequency of separate evaluations should depend primarily on the assessment of risks and the effectiveness of ongoing monitoring procedures. Separate evaluations may take the form of self-assessments as well as review of control design and direct testing of internal control."

[36] The *Government Auditing Standards,* the *Quality Standards for Investigation and Evaluation,* and the *Quality Standards for Inspections* all address supervision of the work process.

internal controls, depending on the risk associated with the activity.

3. *Independent external reviews* are conducted by sources not assigned to the unit being reviewed. These reviews are distinct from ongoing management and supervision, and encompass the entirety of internal control, including administrative operations and professional services (audits, investigations, inspections, and evaluations). Quality assurance is intended to assess the internal controls of the entire OIG or specific OIG components. The Quality Assurance Program is a type of independent review that focuses on complying with professional standards in conducting professional services (see the Maintaining Quality Assurance standard).

V. Maintaining Quality Assurance

A. General Standard[37]

Each OIG shall establish and maintain a quality assurance program to ensure that work performed adheres to established OIG policies and procedures; meets established standards of performance, including applicable professional standards; and is carried out economically, efficiently, and effectively.

External quality assurance reviews provide OIGs with added assurance regarding their adherence to prescribed standards, regulations, and legislation through a formal objective assessment of OIG operations. OIGs are strongly encouraged to have external quality assurance reviews of audits, investigations, inspections, evaluations, and other OIG activities. Each OIG shall participate in the external quality assurance review programs required by statute or applicable authority[38] and implemented through CIGIE guidelines.

B. Quality Assurance Program

Because OIGs evaluate how well agency programs and operations are functioning, they have a special responsibility to ensure that their own operations are as effective as possible. The nature and extent of an OIG's quality assurance program depends on a number of factors, such as the OIG size, the degree of operating autonomy allowed its personnel and its offices, the nature of its work, its organizational structure, and

---

[37] This standard is based on the *Standards for Internal Control in the Federal Government* and the quality control and assurance standard in the *Government Auditing Standards* (Section 3.49).

[38] The IG Act of 1978, as amended, GAGAS, and the *Attorney General Guidelines for Offices of Inspector General with Statutory Law Enforcement Authority*.

appropriate cost-benefit considerations. Thus, the program established by individual OIGs could vary, as could the extent of their documentation. Each organization, however, should prepare appropriate documentation to demonstrate compliance with its policies and procedures for its system of quality assurance.

1. The quality assurance program is an evaluative effort conducted by reviewers external to the units/personnel being reviewed to ensure that the overall work of the OIG meets appropriate standards. The quality assurance program has an internal and external component.

2. The internal quality assurance program can include reviews of all aspects of the OIG's operations. The reviews should be conducted by internal OIG staff that are external to the units being reviewed. The internal quality assurance program is distinct from regular management and supervisory activities, comparisons, and other activities by OIG staff performing their duties. Thus, an audit supervisor ensuring that audit reports are properly referenced to working papers is an example of regular supervision whereas an independent reviewer evaluating the referencing process is an example of internal quality assurance.

3. External quality assurance reviews are conducted by independent organizations not affiliated with the OIG being reviewed.

C. Elements of an Internal Quality Assurance Program

1. An internal quality assurance program must be structured and implemented to ensure an objective, timely, and comprehensive appraisal of operations. The

internal quality assurance reviews should be conducted by individuals who are not directly involved in the activity or unit being reviewed and who do not report to the immediate supervisor of that activity or unit.

2. The same professional care should be taken with quality assurance reviews as with other OIG efforts, including adequately planning the review, documenting findings, developing supportable recommendations, and soliciting comments from the supervisor of the activity or unit reviewed.

3. The IG shall implement necessary improvements on a timely basis.

D. Elements of an External Quality Assurance Program

1. The purpose of the external quality assurance program is to provide an additional and external level of assurance that the OIG conducts its audits, investigations, inspections, and evaluations in compliance with applicable professional standards.

2. The objective of the external quality assurance review is to determine whether the internal control system is in place and operating effectively to provide reasonable assurance that established policies and procedures and applicable professional standards are being followed.

3. Organizations and individuals managing and conducting external quality assurance reviews should be highly qualified and comply with specific supplemental guidance issued by CIGIE to ensure the highest level of review quality. Individuals conducting these reviews should have a thorough knowledge of the applicable professional standards and the environment relative to the work being performed.

4. The reviewers should be independent of the organization being reviewed, its staff, and the work selected for review.

5. The reviewers should have knowledge related to performing an external quality assurance review and use professional judgment in conducting and reporting on the results of the review.

6. The review should be sufficiently comprehensive to assess whether the internal quality assurance program meets its objectives.

7. The external reviewers and the organization under review should prepare and sign a memorandum of understanding regarding fundamental aspects of the review. Possible topics include scope; staffing and time frames; discussion of preliminary findings; reporting; handling of requests for reports, letters of comment, and review documentation; and procedures to address disagreements on findings and recommendations.

8. OIGs should provide copies of final reports resulting from external quality assurance reviews consistent with the guidance provided in the *Guide for Conducting External Peer Reviews of the Audit Organizations of Federal Offices of Inspector General*, p. 23 (May 2009),[39] the *Qualitative Assessment Review Guidelines for Investigative Operations of Federal Offices of Inspectors General*, p. 17 (December 2011),[40] and other appropriate guidance.

---

[39] Commonly referred to as the "Audit Peer Review Guide," available at http://www.ignet.gov/pande/audit/eprps09.pdf.

[40] Commonly referred to as the "Investigations Peer Review Guide," available at http:// www.ignet.gov/pande/standards/invprg1211.pdf.

9. OIGs should have procedures in place to address findings and recommendations contained in external quality assurance reviews.

10. The external quality assurance program can be extended to cover other OIG operations, such as human resources management, procurement or budget operations.

VI. Planning and Coordinating

A. General Standard

Each OIG shall maintain a planning system assessing the nature, scope, and inherent risks of agency programs and operations. This assessment forms the basis for establishing strategic and performance plans,[41] including goals, objectives, and performance measures to be accomplished by the OIG within a specific time period.[42]

The IG and OIG staff shall coordinate their activities internally and with other components of government to assure effective and efficient use of available resources.[43]

---

[41] The GPRA Modernization Act of 2010, Section 2, requires each agency to develop a 5-year strategic plan, and, in Sections 3 and 4, to prepare annual performance plans and reports. A January 28, 1998 memorandum from OMB to the PCIE and the National Science Foundation OIG requires each OIG that has a separate line item account in the President's Budget Appendix to submit a performance plan. The OIGs can either include goals, objectives, and measures in their agency's strategic and performance plans or develop their own strategic and annual performance plans and performance reports.

[42] OMB Circular No. A-123, *Management's Responsibility for Internal Control*, Section 2, states that management accountability is the expectation that managers are responsible for the quality and timeliness of program performance, increasing productivity, controlling costs and mitigating adverse aspects of agency operations, and ensuring that programs are managed with integrity and in compliance with applicable law.

[43] The IG Act charges the IGs with broad responsibility for coordinating various enforcement and oversight activities within their agencies, and between their agencies and others. Specifically, IGs are to "conduct, supervise or coordinate the following activities: audits and investigations relating to the programs and operations of the agency (5 U.S.C. app. 3 § 4(a)(1)); other activities carried out or financed by the agency for the purpose of promoting economy and efficiency or preventing and

B. Elements of the Planning Process

OIGs should develop an appropriate planning process, giving consideration to the following elements.

1. Use a strategic planning process that carefully considers current and emerging agency programs, operations, risks, and management challenges. This analysis will identify and assess the nature of agency programs and operations, their performance measures and anticipated outcomes, their scope and dollar magnitude, their staffing and budgetary trends, their perceived vulnerabilities, and their inherent risks.

2. Develop a methodology and process for identifying and prioritizing agency programs and operations as potential subjects for audit, investigation, inspection, or evaluation. The methodology should be designed to use the most effective combination of OIG resources, including previous OIG work and input from OIG staff. Also, the OIG should consider the plans of other organizations both internal and external to the agency.

3. Use an annual performance planning process that identifies the activities to audit, investigate, inspect, or evaluate and translates these priorities into outcome-related goals, objectives, and performance measures. As part of this planning process, OIGs should consider

---

detecting fraud and abuse in its programs and operations (5 U.S.C. app. 3 § 4(a)(3)); and relationships between the agency and other Federal agencies, State and local governments, and nongovernmental entities with respect to (A) all matters relating to promoting economy and efficiency or preventing and detecting fraud and abuse in programs and operations administered or financed by the agency or (B) identifying and prosecuting participants in such fraud or abuse (5 U.S.C. app. 3 § 4(a)(4)).

agency actions to address recommendations from prior OIG work. Because resources are rarely sufficient to meet requirements, the OIG must choose among competing needs.

C. Coordination Considerations

1. In planning work, the OIG should coordinate, where applicable, with agency management to ensure that OIG priorities appropriately consider agency needs. The OIG should take into consideration requests from the Congress, the OMB, other external stakeholders, the CIGIE, complaints from employees and, as appropriate, private citizens. By using this information, along with the OIG's knowledge of agency objectives and operations, the OIG can plan its work based on the relative costs and benefits.

2. The OIG should minimize duplicative work. The OIG should coordinate its work internally and with other groups (both inside and outside the agency) performing independent evaluations of agency operations and programs. This coordination should identify the nature and scope of other reviews, both planned and completed, to avoid duplicating others' work. Coordinating with the GAO is particularly important. As part of the planning process, each OIG should coordinate as needed with GAO representatives to exchange and discuss tentative plans for the next fiscal year.[44] If duplication is identified, every effort should be made to resolve it.

3. The OIG will closely coordinate with the Department of Justice with respect to criminal and civil investigations

---

[44] 5 U.S.C. app. 3 § 4(c).

in compliance with the *Attorney General Guidelines for Offices of Inspector General with Statutory Law Enforcement Authority*, the CIGIE *Quality Standards for Investigations*, and other guidelines, as applicable.

4. When OIG staff identifies problems that might affect other offices, agencies, or arms of government, the OIG should coordinate with them and their respective OIGs. Where appropriate, joint or coordinated audits, investigations, inspections, or evaluations may be performed to address the respective interests of the various agencies and offices. [45]

5. Because of the close interrelationships among many Federal programs, situations will arise where audit, investigation, inspection, or evaluation activity by one OIG will require work with another agency's program or administrative staff. In such cases, the OIGs will coordinate in order to facilitate the efficient accomplishment of the work.

---

[45] 5 U.S.C. app. 3 § 11 establishes the Council of the Inspectors General on Integrity and Efficiency. Among the responsibilities of the Council is to identify, review, and discuss areas of weakness and vulnerability in Federal programs and operations to fraud, waste, and abuse, and to develop plans for coordinated, Government-wide activities that address these problems and promote economy and efficiency in Federal programs and operations. These activities will include interagency and inter-entity audit and investigation programs and projects to deal efficiently and effectively with those problems concerning fraud and waste that exceed the capability or jurisdiction of an individual agency or entity. The Council shall recognize the preeminent role of the Department of Justice in law enforcement and litigation.

D. Prevention

OIG planning should include a strategy to identify the causes of fraud, waste, abuse, and mismanagement in high-risk agency programs, and to help agencies implement a system of management improvements to overcome these problems.[46] OIG prevention efforts may include the following:

1. A routine procedure for OIG staff to identify and report prevention opportunities as these may come up in their work, and for OIG managers to refer these to agency management, as appropriate;

2. Special awareness and training initiatives designed to alert agency employees to systemic weaknesses in the programs and operations of their agencies;

3. Review and comment on initial design of new agency programs and operations;

4. Analyses of audit, investigative, and other OIG reports to identify trends and patterns;

5. Education and training to ensure that appropriate OIG staff have requisite abilities in the loss prevention area, as well as fraud detection and prevention; and

6. An effective means for tracking the implementation of recommendations.

---

[46] 5 U.S.C. app. 3 § 4(a)(3) makes it the duty and responsibility of each OIG "to recommend policies for, and to conduct, supervise, or coordinate other activities...for the purpose of...preventing and detecting fraud and abuse."

VII. Communicating Results of OIG Activities

A. General Standard

Each OIG shall keep agency management, program managers, and the Congress fully and currently informed of appropriate aspects of OIG operations and findings. OIGs should assess and report to the Congress, as appropriate, on their own strategic and annual performance and the performance of the agency or department for which they have cognizance. Each OIG shall also report expeditiously to the Attorney General whenever the IG has reasonable grounds to believe there has been a violation of Federal criminal law.

B. Keeping the Head of the Agency Informed[47]

1. Through periodic briefings and reports, the IG should keep the appropriate department and agency heads advised of important undertakings of the OIG, its outcomes, and any problems encountered that warrant the department or agency head's attention.

2. The IG should timely advise department and agency heads of any agency official who attempts to impede or fails to require a contractor under his or her responsibility to desist from impeding an audit, investigation, inspection, evaluation, or any other OIG activity.[48]

---

[47] 5 U.S.C. app. 3 §§ 4(a)(5) and 5(b), require that OIGs keep the head of the establishment and the Congress fully and currently informed about problems and deficiencies relating to the administration of programs and operations and the necessity for and progress of corrective action.

[48] 5 U.S.C. app. 3 § 6(b)(2).

3. The IG should timely alert department and agency heads, consistent with requirements imposed by confidentiality and the prosecutive system, to examples of egregious misconduct and waste.

C. Keeping the Congress Informed

1. The IG shall report to the Congress semiannually, as required by the IG Act of 1978, as amended, and other legislation, regulations, and directives.

2. When an IG becomes aware of a particularly serious or flagrant problem, abuse or deficiency relating to the administration of the programs or operations of their agency, the IG shall immediately notify the head of the agency of that problem, abuse or deficiency. The agency head must then, within seven calendar days, transmit to the appropriate committees in Congress any such report of the IG, as well as any agency's comments. (5 U.S.C. app. 3 § 5(d).

3. If the results of an audit, investigation, inspection, or evaluation indicate that deficiencies in Federal law contribute to fraud, waste, or abuse, these matters may be brought to the attention of the Congress, and may include recommendations for statutory change.[49]

4. The IG shall also report to the Congress and OMB on management challenges facing the agency or department and progress in meeting the challenges.[50]

---

[49] *Id.* at § 4(a)(2).

[50] 31 U.S.C. § 3516(d) requires OIGs to summarize what the IG considers to be the most serious management and performance challenges facing the IG's agency and briefly assess the agency's progress in addressing

5. The Inspector General may inform the agency head and Congress using other appropriate means concerning fraud and other serious problems, abuses, and deficiencies relating to the agency's programs and operations. (5 U.S.C. app. 3 § 4(a)(5)

D. Keeping the Congress and Agency Informed on Performance

1. Each OIG should annually assess its own performance by evaluating actual to planned performance.

2. Each OIG should have sufficient information to conduct performance evaluations, e.g., a history of past results to show prior performance, a strategic and annual planning process to show expected performance, and a management information system to show actual performance.

3. Each OIG should report annually on its actual performance as compared to its performance goals, either as a contributing part of their agency reporting under the Government Performance and Results Act of 1993 (GPRA), if appropriate, or independently to their agency and Congress.

4. IGs may also advise the Congress on the performance goals, measurement process, and results of the agencies and departments for which they have cognizance.

E. Keeping Program Managers Informed

The OIG should make a special and continuing effort to keep program managers and their key staff informed, if appropriate,

---

those challenges. This requirement is triggered by the agency's consolidation of reports made to the Congress, OMB, or the President.

about the purpose, nature, and content of OIG activity associated with the manager's programs. These efforts may include periodic briefings as well as interim reports and correspondence.

F. Keeping Ethics Officials Informed

The OIG should make a special and continuing effort to keep the Designated Agency Ethics Official or similar official informed about OIG activities, including the results of investigations and allegations of ethical misconduct where appropriate, that related to the ethics official's responsibilities for the agency's ethics program.

G. Keeping the Attorney General Informed[51]

OIGs must report expeditiously to the Department of Justice whenever they have reasonable grounds to believe there has been a violation of Federal criminal law.

H. Keeping the Public Informed

The OIG shall make its semiannual reports available to the public.[52] The OIG shall, not later than 3 days after any report or audit is made publicly available post that report or audit on the OIG's website.[53]

Each OIG shall ensure that their respective department or agency prominently maintains a direct link to the OIG's website on the agency's homepage. The OIG shall also establish a link to report fraud, waste and abuse on its

---

[51] 5 U.S.C. app. 3 § 4(d).

[52] *Id.* at § 5(c).

[53] *Id.* at § 8L(b).

homepage. Each OIG shall provide a service on its website to allow an individual to request automatic receipt of information relating to any public report or audit, or portion thereof, and which permits electronic transmittal of the information, or notice of the availability of the information without further request.[54]

I. Elements of Effective Reporting[55]

1. All products issued should comply with applicable professional standards and conform to the OIG's established policies and procedures.

2. Whether written or oral, all OIG reports should be objective, timely, and useful.

3. All products should be adequately supported.

---

[54] *Id.* at § 8L(a)

[55] OMB *Guidelines for Ensuring and Maximizing the Quality, Objectivity, Utility, and Integrity of Information Disseminated by Federal Agencies* require agencies to adopt a basic standard of information quality (including objectivity, utility, and integrity) as a performance goal and take appropriate steps to incorporate information quality criteria into agency information dissemination practices. Quality is to be ensured and established at levels appropriate to the nature and timeliness of the information to be disseminated. Agencies shall adopt specific standards of quality that are appropriate for the various categories of information they disseminate, and, as a matter of good and effective agency information resources management, agencies are to develop a process for reviewing the quality (including the objectivity, utility, and integrity) of information before it is disseminated. The *Government Auditing Standards*, the *Quality Standards for Investigations*, and the *Quality Standards for Inspection and Evaluation* all address reporting standards for individual audit, investigative, and inspection or evaluation reports.

VIII. Managing Human Capital

A. General Standard[56]

Each OIG should have a process to ensure that the OIG's staff members collectively possess the core competencies needed to accomplish the OIG mission.

B. Human Capital Processes

Each OIG's process for ensuring that its staff members possess the requisite qualifications should encompass processes for recruiting, hiring, continuously developing, training, and evaluating their staff members, and succession planning to assist the organization in maintaining a workforce that has the ability to meet the OIG's mission.

C. Core Competencies

Staff members must collectively possess the professional competence (i.e., teamwork, leadership, communication,

---

[56] The *Standards for Internal Control in the Federal Government* identifies one factor affecting the control environment as management's commitment to competence. All personnel need to possess and maintain a level of competence that allows them to accomplish their assigned duties, as well as understand the importance of developing and implementing good internal control. Management needs to identify what appropriate knowledge and skills are needed for various jobs and provide training as well as candid and constructive counseling, and performance appraisals. The Standards also discuss good human capital policies and practices as another critical environmental factor. This includes establishing appropriate practices for hiring, orienting, training, evaluating, counseling, promoting, compensating, and disciplining personnel. The IG Reform Act provides that CICIE "maintain 1 or more academies as the Council considers desirable for the professional training of auditors, investigators, inspectors, evaluators and other personnel of the various Offices of Inspector General."

technical knowledge, critical thinking skills, abilities, and experience) to perform the work assigned. In addition, staff must individually meet requirements established by the Office of Personnel Management for their respective job series and by applicable professional standards.

D. Skills Assessment

To ensure that the OIG staff members collectively possess needed skills, the IG and key managers should assess the skills of their staff members and determine the extent to which these skills match the OIG's requirements. OIG management is responsible for deciding the methods by which identified needs can be met by hiring contractors or outside consultants, using staff members who possess the requisite skills, developing staff members and providing training, or recruiting new staff. Each OIG must also ensure that staff members meet the requirements for continuing professional education contained in the applicable professional standards.[57]

---

[57] The *Government Auditing Standards,* the *Quality Standards for Investigations*, and the *Quality Standards for Inspection and Evaluation* each require that the personnel collectively possess the skills and abilities to perform the assigned tasks and require continuing professional education.

IX. Reviewing Legislation and Regulations

A. General Standard

Each OIG shall establish and maintain a system to review and comment on existing and proposed legislation, regulations, and those directives that affect both the programs and operations of the OIG's agency or the mission and functions of the OIG.[58] The system should result in OIG recommendations designed to (1) promote economy and efficiency in administering agency programs and operations; (2) prevent and detect fraud and abuse in such programs and operations; and (3) protect the integrity and independence of the OIG.

B. Elements of Legislative and Regulatory Review

1. OIGs should assure independent and timely formulation and transmission of OIG recommendations so that authorities dealing with the matters concerned can adequately consider the OIG comments. This requires early identification of legislative, regulatory, and those key administrative or directive issues of particular interest to the OIG.

2. OIGs should seek implementation of agency procedures that routinely provide for OIG review or comment on legislative and regulatory proposals of interest to the OIG and on agency-wide directives.

---

[58] 5 U.S.C. app. 3 § 4(a)(2), gives IGs the responsibility to review existing and proposed legislation and regulations and make recommendations in the semiannual reports on the impact of legislation or regulations on the economy and efficiency of administering the agency's programs and operations or in preventing and detecting fraud and abuse.

3. OIGs should have written procedures for and conduct appropriate reviews, as necessary, of authorizing legislation, regulations, and directives during investigations, audits, inspections and evaluations, and other OIG activities, particularly when it appears that a lack of controls or deficiencies in law have contributed to fraud, waste, abuse, and mismanagement.

X. Receiving and Reviewing Allegations

A. General Standard[59]

Each OIG shall establish and follow policies and procedures for receiving and reviewing allegations. This system should ensure that an appropriate disposition, including appropriate notification, is made for each allegation.

B. Elements of a System for Receiving and Reviewing Allegations

This system should ensure that:

1. The OIG has a well-publicized mechanism through which agency employees and other interested persons can submit allegations of fraud, waste, abuse, and mismanagement.

2. The OIG's website has a direct link on the homepage for individuals to submit allegations. Those using the direct link shall not be required to provide personally identifiable information.

3. The OIG shall not disclose the identity of an individual who submits allegations through the OIG's website link without the consent of the individual, unless the OIG determines such disclosure is unavoidable during the course of the investigation. [60] Concerning agency employees who provide information or complaints to their OIG, the OIG shall not disclose the identity of such employees without their consent, unless the OIG determines such disclosure is unavoidable during the

---

[59] *Id.* at §§ 7 and 8L.
[60] *Id.* at § 8L.

course of the investigation, regardless of whether the information or complaint was submitted through the OIG website.[61]

4. Each allegation is retrievable and its receipt, review, and disposition are documented.

5. Each allegation is initially screened to ensure that urgent and/or high priority matters receive timely attention and facilitate early determination of the appropriate courses of action for those complaints requiring follow-up action.

6. Based on the nature, content, and credibility of the complaint, allegations are appropriately reviewed.

C. Feedback

The OIG may establish a mechanism for providing feedback to parties who submit allegations. This feedback can be furnished in summary form through such vehicles as an employee newsletter, a semiannual report digest, or other means.

---

[61] *Id.* at § 7.

Legislation, Executive Orders, Standards, and OMB and Other Guidance Impacting the IG Community

Document[a]	Description
Legislation	
The IG Act , 5 U.S.C. App. 3 (P.L. 95-452)	Establishes independent and objective Offices of IG. Requires IGs to report violations of criminal law to the Attorney General, as also required by 28 U.S.C. § 535. Amended 1988 & 2008.
Notable amendments to the IG Act: 1988, 2002, 2008	1988 Amendment (P.L. 100-504): Primary change: created IGs for the Department of Justice and Department of Treasury, as well as smaller agencies.
	2002 Amendment (see the Homeland Security Act, below).
	2008 Amendment (P.L. 110-409): Significant changes: combined former President's Council on Integrity and Efficiency ("PCIE") and Executive Council on Integrity and Efficiency ("ECIE") into a single, statutory Council of the Inspectors General on Integrity and Efficiency ("CIGIE"), and provided CIGIE with added resources and structure; required IGs to post reports online; required IGs to have anonymous complaint "hotlines" available on their websites; expressly included data and other electronic information in IG subpoena power; gave IGs legal

Document[a]	Description
	counsel independence from their establishments.
Accounting and Auditing Act of 1950, 31 U.S.C. §§713, 714, 718, 719, 3326, 3501, 3511-3514, 3521, 3523, 3524 (P.L. 97-258)	Requires the head of each executive agency to certify that the agency's systems for internal accounting and administrative control comply with standards prescribed by the Comptroller General.
Anti-deficiency Act, 31 U.S.C. § 1341	Forbids agencies from using appropriated money for unauthorized purposes or timeframes.
Budget and Accounting Act of 1921, 31 U.S.C. §§ 501, 502, 521, 522, 701-704, 711, 712, 716, 718, 719, 731, 771-779, 1101, 1104-1108, 1111, 1113, 3301, 3323, 3324, 3521, 3522, 3526, 3529, 3531, 3541, 3702. (42 Stat. 20)	Assigns responsibilities for government accounting, auditing, and financial reporting to improve evaluations of Federal Government programs and activities by better identifying sources of funding and how the funding was applied.
Dodd-Frank Wall Street Reform and Consumer Protection Act, 12 U.S.C. §§ 5301-5641 (P.L. 111-203)	Some sections, including 12 U.S.C. § 5437, and P.L 111-203 §§ 989B, 989C, 989D, and 989E, affect certain IGs and IG functions.
Federal Financial Management Act of 1994, 31 U.S.C. §§ 331, 501 note, 3301 note, 3332, 3515, 3521. (P.L. 103-356)	Requires all agencies covered by the Chief Financial Officers Act to prepare annual, agency wide financial statements.
Federal Financial Management Improvement Act of 1996, 5 U.S.C. App §5; 10 U.S.C.§§ 113 note, 2315; 15 U.S.C. §278g-3; 28 U.S.C. §612; 31 U.S.C. §§ 3512, 3512 note, 3521; 38 U.S.C. §310; 40 U.S.C. §§ 1401 notes, 1441 note; 41 U.S.C. § 251 notes.(P.L. 104-208)	Provides for the establishment of uniform Federal Government accounting systems, accounting standards, and reporting systems.

Document[a]	Description
Federal Information Security Management Act of 2002, 44 U.S.C. § 3541, et seq. (P.L. 107-347)	Mandates stricter computer and network security, including yearly security audits
Federal Managers Financial Integrity Act of 1982, 31 U.S.C. §§1105, 1113, 3512. (P.L. 97-255)	Provides for establishment, implementation, and evaluation of accounting and administrative controls regarding financial management activities.
Government Performance and Results Modernization Act of 2010, 5 U.S.C. § 306; 31 U.S.C. §§ 1101 note, 1105, 1115, 1115 note, 1116-1119, 9703, 9704; 39 U.S.C. §§ 2801-2805. (P.L. 103-62)	Provides for the establishment of strategic planning and performance measurement in the Federal Government.
Government Management Reform Act of 1994, 2 U.S.C. § 31, 31 note; 3 U.S.C. § 104; 5 U.S.C. §§ 5318, 6304, 6304 note; 28 U.S.C. § 461; 31 U.S.C. §§ 331 note, 501 note, 1113 note, 3301 note, 3332, 3515, 3521. (P.L. 103-356)	Improves the efficiency of executive branch performance by enhancing reporting to the Congress through elimination and consolidation of duplicative or obsolete reporting requirements.
Homeland Security Act of 2002 (P.L. 107-296)	Gives OIGs law enforcement powers, such as the power to make arrests and carry firearms, subject to Attorney General Guidelines.
Improper Payments Elimination and Recovery Act of 2010, 31 U.S.C. § 3301, et seq. (P.L. 111-204)	Seeks to reduce wasteful and improper government payments by requiring agency heads to review their programs and activities for those that may be susceptible to significant improper payments.
Chief Financial Officers Act of 1990, 5 U.S.C. §§ 5313-5315; 31 U.S.C. §§ 501 notes, 502-506, 901, 901 notes, 902, 903, 1105, 3511 note, 3512, 3515, 3515 note, 3521, 3521 note, 9105, 9106; 38 U.S.C. § 201 note; 42 U.S.C. § 3533. (P.L. 101-576)	Improves the general and financial management of the Federal Government.

Document[a]	Description
E-Government Act of 2002, 5 U.S.C. §§ 3111, 3701-3707, 4108, 8432 note; 10 U.S.C. §§ 2224, 2332; 13 U.S.C. § 402; 15 U.S.C. §§ 176a, 278g-3, 278g-4; 18 U.S.C. §§ 207, 209; 28 U.S.C. § 1913 note; 31 U.S.C. §§ 503, 507; 40 U.S.C. §§ 305, 502, 11331, 11332, 11501-11505, 11521, 11522; 41 U.S.C. §§ 266a, 423; 44 U.S.C. §§ 101 note, 3501, 3504-3506, 3531, 3541-3549, 3601-3606. (P.L. 107-347)	Provides for the independent review of Federal agency information technology security by Offices of IG. Was amended in 2004 to include a section on privacy and security concerns.

Document[a]	Description
Clinger-Cohen Act of 1996, 5 U.S.C. § 571 note, 5315; 5 U.S.C. App 3 § 11, 11 note; 10 U.S.C. §§ 1701 note, 2220, 2249, 2302, 2304, 2304 note, 2304e, 2305, 2305a, 2306a, 2306 note, 2306b, 2315, 2323, 2324, 2350b, 2372, 2384, 2397, 2397a-2397c, 2400, 2401 note, 2405, 2409, 2410, 2410b, 2410d, 2410g, 2424, 2431, 2432 note, 2461, 2533, 2539b, 2662, 2702; 15 U.S.C. §§ 278g-3, 637, 644, 789; 16 U.S.C. § 799; 18 U.S.C. § 281; 22 U.S.C. § 2761, 2761 note; 28 U.S.C. § 612; 29 U.S.C. § 721; 31 U.S.C. §§ 1352, 1558, 3551-3554; 38 U.S.C. § 310; see 40 U.S.C. §§ 11101-11103, 11301-11303, 11311-11318, 11331, 11332, 11501-11505, 11521, 11522, 11701-11704; 41 U.S.C. §§ 10a note, 11, 15, 20a, 20b, 22, 35 note, 43a, 43b, 44, 45, 57, 251 note, 253, 253a, 253b, 253l, 253m, 254b, 254d, 255, 257, 264a, 265, 266, 401-434, 601, 605, 612, 701; 42 U.S.C. §§ 6392, (P.L. 104-156)	Provides for OMB oversight of information technology development and acquisition, agency management of IT investments, and establishment of standards by NIST.
Notification and Federal Employee Antidiscrimination and Retaliation Act of 2002 (No FEAR Act) (P.L. 107-174)	Some sections, including 12 U.S.C. § 5437, and P.L 111-203 §§ 989B, 989C, 989D, and 989E, affect certain IGs and IG functions.
Paperwork Reduction Act of 1980, as amended, 44 U.S.C. §§ 3501-20, (P.L. 96-511)	Restricts some agency requests for information from the public; sometimes relevant to audits, evaluations, and other IG attempts to gather information.

Document[a]	Description
Reports Consolidation Act of 2000, 31 U.S.C. §§ 3116, 3501 note, 3515, 3516, 3521. (P.L. 106-531)	Encourages and authorizes report consolidation; makes report formats more useful and meaningful; improves the quality of information reported; enhances the coordination and efficiency of such reports.
Single Audit Act Amendments of 1996, 31 U.S.C. §§ 7501, 7501 notes, 7502-7505. (P.L. 104-156)	Requires that the *Government Auditing Standards* be followed in audits of state and local governments and nonprofit entities that receive federal financial assistance. OMB Circular A-133 implemented this Act.
Privacy Act, 5 U.S.C. §552(a), as amended (P.L. 93-579)	Places limitations on how federal agencies collect, use, and disclose information about individuals (U.S. citizens and resident aliens). Gives individuals the right to have access to records maintained on them by agencies and the right to seek corrections to those records, subject to various exemptions. Amended in 2004.
Freedom of Information Act, as amended, 5 U.S.C. §552, (P.L. 104-231)	Holds the government accountable to the governed; it establishes a statutory right, enforceable in court, for persons (individuals, corporations, etc.) to have access to Federal agency records, subject to certain exemptions.
Whistleblower Protection Act, 5 U.S.C. §§ 1201, 1201 notes, 1202-1206, 1208, 1209, 1211, 1211 note, 1212-1219, 1221, 1222, 2302, 2303, 3352, 3393, 5509 notes, 7502, 7512, 7521, 7542, 7701, 7703; 22 U.S.C. § 4139	Protects the rights of, and prevents reprisals against, Federal employees who disclose governmental fraud, waste, abuse, and other types of corruption or illegality.

Document[a]	Description
Health Insurance Portability and Accountability Act (PL 104-191)	Covers the privacy of individually-identifiable information.
Trade Secrets Act, 18 U.S.C. § 1905	Prohibits OIGs from disclosing confidential proprietary data obtained during the course of conducting their work unless such disclosure is authorized by law.
Federal Conflict of Interest Laws, 18 U.S.C. §§ 201-209	Establishes criminal prohibitions for employees of the Executive Branch.

Document[a]	Description
Executive Orders	
Integrity and Efficiency in Federal Programs, Exec. Order No. 12805, 57 FR 20627 (May 11, 1992)	Establishes the PCIE and ECIE and describes their functions and responsibilities. (Note: PCIE and ECIE were merged to create CIGIE.)
Administrative Allegations Against Inspectors General, Exec. Order No. 12993, 61 FR 13043 (March 21, 1996)	Provided that the PCIE and ECIE Integrity Committee shall receive, review, and refer for investigation allegations of wrongdoing against IGs and certain staff members of OIGs. (Note: PCIE and ECIE were merged to create CIGIE.)
Ethics Commitments by Executive Branch Personnel, Exec. Order No.13490 (Jan 21, 2009)	Requires executive agency employees appointed on or after Jan. 20, 2009 to sign a new ethics pledge that, among other things, imposes stronger restrictions on contact with lobbyists and work on prior, private-sector matters.
Delivering an Efficient, Effective, and Accountable Government, Exec Order No. 13575 (June 13, 2011)	Aims to advance efforts to detect and remediate fraud, waste, and abuse in federal programs, and to eliminate wasteful or otherwise inefficient programs. Creates the Government Accountability and Transparency Board to complement the Recovery Accountability and Transparency Board.
Classified National Security Information, Exec. Order No. 13526 (Dec. 29, 2009)	Permits the federal government to reclassify information as relevant to national security after the information has been requested.
Attorney General Guidelines for Offices of IG with Statutory Law Enforcement Authority (Dec. 8, 2003)	Provides enumerated IGs with law enforcement powers. Sets forth rules for those IGs' use of their law enforcement powers.

Document[a]	Description
Attorney General Memorandum for Heads of Executive Departments and Agencies Re: The Freedom of Information Act (March 19, 2009)	Creates a new "presumption of openness" for FOIA requests, stating that the Department of Justice will defend a denial of a FOIA request only if the denying agency reasonably foresees harm from disclosure or the disclosure is prohibited by law.
Standards	
Standards for Internal Control in the Federal Government, GAO/AIMD-00-21.3.1	Establishes overall framework for establishing and maintaining internal control and for identifying and addressing major performance and management challenges and areas at greatest risk of fraud, waste, abuse, and mismanagement.
Government Auditing Standards ("Yellow Book") ("Generally Accepted Government Auditing Standards") ("GAGAS") (2011 ed.)	Provides uniform rules and standards for federal government audits. Multiple revisions made in 2011.
Quality Standards for Investigations, CIGIE (2011 ed.)	Establishes standards for investigative efforts conducted by criminal investigators working for Offices of IG.
Quality Standards for Inspection and Evaluation ("Blue Book"), CIGIE (2011 ed.)	Establishes standards for inspections and evaluations conducted by federal agencies.
Standards of Ethical Conduct for Employees of the Executive Branch, 5 C.F.R. Part 2635	Establishes general principles for ethical conduct of employees of the Executive Branch.

Document[a]	Description
Statements of Federal Financial Accounting Concepts and Standards, Federal Accounting Standards Advisory Board (June 2009)	Accounting principles for Federal government reporting entities issued by the Federal Accounting Standards Advisory Board.
Codification of Statements on Auditing Standards (Including Statements on Standards for Attestation Engagements), American Institute of Certified Public Accountants (2011)	Auditing standards for financial audits.

OMB Circulars, Bulletins, Memoranda, and Guidance

Various OMB Circulars, Bulletins, Memoranda, and Guidance applicable to OIG work, including but not limited to, OMB Memorandum No. 06-15, Safeguarding Personally Identifiable Information, and OMB Memorandum No. 06-16, Protection of Sensitive Agency Information, as well as Circular A-76, "Performance of Commercial Activities;" A-102, "Grants and Cooperative Agreements with State and Local Governments;" and A-123, "Management's Responsibility for Internal Control." Listed by category under "Information for Agencies" atwww.whitehouse.gov/omb	Establish requirements and guidelines for implementing: ▪ internal controls ▪ management accountability and control ▪ federal financial systems ▪ management of federal information resources ▪ audits of states, local governments and non-profit organizations ▪ financial accounting principles and standards ▪ financial statement audits ▪ information dissemination

Other Guidance

Guide for Conducting External Quality Control Reviews of the Audit Operations of the Offices of IG, CIGIE (March 2009)	Provides guidance on conducting external quality control reviews of OIG Offices of Audit.

Document[a]	Description
Qualitative Assessment Review Guidelines for Investigative Operations of Federal Offices of IG, CIGIE (December 2011)	Provides guidance on conducting external qualitative assessment reviews of OIG investigative operations.
Principles of Federal Appropriations Law ("GAO Redbook")	Multi-volume treatise setting forth myriad rules for spending and allocating federal funds, as established by court cases, legislation, and Comptroller General decisions.
Department of Justice Office of Information Policy, Freedom of Information Act Guidance. www.justice.gov/oip/oip-guidance.html	Comprehensive resource for FOIA compliance and policy, including the 2009 Guide to the Freedom of Information Act, available at www.justice.gov/oip/foia_guide09.htm.
GAO Financial Audit Manual	Provides guidance on conducting financial statement audits.

---

[a] Some OIGs are not components of an entity legally defined as a "Federal agency." Therefore, some of the cited laws, regulations, or other guidance may not be directly applicable by law to all OIGs. In these cases, principles or concepts in the laws, regulations, or other guidance may be adopted by the OIG entities as a matter of policy.

Members of the CIGIE Professional Development Committee Who Participated in Revising the Quality Standards for Federal Offices of IG

Mary L. Kendall, Chair
Department of the Interior

Lynne A. McFarland, Vice Chair
Federal Election Commission

Ted Alves
AMTRAK

David L. Hunt
Federal Communications Commission

Daniel R. Levinson
Health and Human Services

Patrick E. McFarland
Office of Personnel Management

Richard Moore
Tennessee Valley Authority

Bruce Delaplaine
Department of the Interior